D1216835

JIGGERY-POKERY

A COMPENDIUM OF

DOUBLE DACTYLS

JIGGERY-POKERY

A COMPENDIUM OF

DOUBLE DACTYLS

EDITED BY

ANTHONY HECHT

AND

JOHN HOLLANDER

DRAWINGS BY MILTON GLASER

ATHENEUM

NEW YORK

1967

Acknowledgments: Thanks are due to Esquire, Inc., in whose magazine some of the double dactyls originally appeared.

FOR W. H. AUDEN

JIGGERY-POKERY

A COMPENDIUM OF

DOUBLE DACTYLS

The General Background

Since the time of the Industrial Revolution at least, perhaps since the seventeenth century—when England's greatest architect, Sir Christopher Wren, was known primarily as an astronomer and member of the Royal Society—prestige, honor and wealth have been heaped upon the general scientific enterprise, and the reverence once reserved for the arts has languished. The more perceptive commentators on modern culture have not failed to notice this; but one turns in vain to Erich Heller or Susan Sontag, for example, for an explanation. No one in our time could gainsay the fact that the scientist has reached the very apogee of his authority, not merely within his own strict purview but as a prophet of our very way of life; while the poet and the artist grow beards, inhabit a slipshod, ersatz Bohemia, and are regarded by the public with detached amusement and suspicion.

The failure of Miss Sontag and Professor Heller to grasp the reasons for this remarkable revolution lies not in the fact that the evidence needed for explanation was deeply and cleverly concealed, but that it was altogether so open and available that it has persistently been ignored. The truth of the matter is simply this: from our earliest school days we associate the great innovations within the scientific domain with warm, human anecdotes about the innovators at the moment of innovation; but this has never been true of the arts.

Let us offer only two of many possible examples. There cannot be a schoolboy in any part of the western world who, when thinking, however fleetingly, about specific gravity, does not instantly conjure in his mind's eye an affectionate image of Archimedes, wet and naked, bucketing giddily about the streets of Syracuse, and shouting "εὕρηκα!" or words to that effect. This is familiar to us all, a part of the universal mental makeup of Western Man (and Boy). The other example will require a little more background and description.

Those who were fortunate enough to have missed the New York World's Fair of 1965–6 will not be able, by dint of however strenuous an effort of imagination, to conceive of the educational exhibit offered by the Bell Telephone Company. One entered this enormous pavilion and was presently established in a comfortable, well-upholstered, wing-backed seat facing the outer wall of the building. The seats were on a slowly moving conveyor belt. Cunningly concealed in the wings of the seat were tiny amplifiers, offering music and instruction, and so synchronized with the passing scene as to describe at all times what was directly before you. Upon one's first sitting down an outfit rather like the Mormon Tabernacle Choir sang a hymn of welcome to the visitor and expressed generally benign sentiments. As one got underway, the choir was dimmed down (though continuing to sing enthusiastically in the background during the entire experience) and a kind, instructional, authoritative voice began to tell about how cave men communicated with each other, as one was conveyed past animated models of cave men in caves, building fires and behaving thoroughly respectably. Naturally, communication got better as time went on; the instructional voice filled with pride, and the choir got rather rapturous.

And then the climactic moment was at hand. There, before one, was Alexander Graham Bell himself, who had just inadvertently and rather clumsily spilled a jar of acid on his work table, thus accidentally providing precisely the electrical circuit that made the telephone work. In his impatience with himself for spilling the acid, the thrilled instructional voice told us, Bell called out, "Dr. Watson, come here. I want you." "These were the seven first words to pass over the telephone," said the instructional voice with reverence, and since it was sort of dark and churchlike, with the choir still plugging away in the background, something of the authority and magnitude of the Seven Last Words of Christ seemed to invest the whole Bell Corporation, to suggest a great synthesis of the Annunciation and Pentecost; and indeed so exalted and transcendental did that moment become that the final effort to push "princess" phones seemed something of an anticlimax.

But the worlds of art and literature present no such richly textured human-interest documents of discovery. No doubt, for instance, the invention of blank verse in English was one of the great and significant innovations in verse form. It has been a matter of convenience to teachers and to literary historians to attribute this innovation to Henry Howard, Earl of Surrey. In his translation of two books of *The Aeneid* Surrey had sought for and found an English equivalent to Virgil's unrhymed Latin. But the attribution could as well be made to Nicholas Grimald and at about the same time. Similarly, Thomas Sackville, Earl of Dorset, and his collaborator Thomas Norton, are credited with introducing blank verse to the English stage in *The Tragedy of Gorboduc* (which Mr. Dodsley insisted on calling *Ferrex and Porrex*, which is like calling *King Lear, Goneril and Regan*) but we have little genuine authority for this, so many plays having been lost, and of course we have no intimate news of its inception. Who invented the sonnet? We simply do not know. Who wrote the first sestina? The matter is not even susceptible of investigation. There is nothing for the young mind to grasp in dramatic terms, and for the adult mind to remember ever after. What poet, in the heat of inspiration, does not wish he were later able to record his discoveries in such a manner as this:

"When I was about to go to bed, an amanuensis of mine, accustomed to make observations, informed me, that one of the servants of the house, going upon some occasion into the larder, was frightened by something of luminous, that she saw (notwithstanding the darkness of the place), where the meat had been hung up before. Whereupon, suspending for a while my going to rest, I presently sent for the meat into my chamber, and caused it to be placed in a corner of the room capable of being made considerably dark, and then I plainly saw, both with wonder and delight, that the joint of meat did, in divers places, shine like rotten wood or stinking fish; which was so uncommon a sight, that I had presently thoughts of inviting you to be a sharer in the pleasure of it. But the late hour of the night did not only make me fear to give you too unseasonable a trouble, but being joined with a great cold, I had got that day by making trial of a new telescope, you saw, in a windy place, I durst not sit up long enough to make all the trials, that I had thought of, and judged the occasion worthy of."

THE HON. ROBERT BOYLE, *Philosophical Works:*
Observations upon Shining Flesh

Except, perhaps, in the cases of Coleridge, whose inspiration was so regrettably interrupted by the person from Porlock, Edgar Allen Poe, whose reliability may be questioned, and Allen Ginsberg, few stories of this sort have been forthcoming from poets and artists. Wagner's celebrated account of how a peculiar kind of trance swept over him to leave in its wake a certain E-flat major triad that would bear the eventual ripe fruit of the orchestral overture to *Das Rheingold* is tedious in the extreme, and the inspirational moments of musical composers have, in recent decades, tended to become assimilated to a *Gestalt* whose earliest discernible elements were Cornel Wilde, Merle Oberon, a Majorca set and some fortuitous raindrops. Even antiquity provides no such anecdotal memorials. Theocritus first employed the epic hexameters for his pastoral idylls; it was perhaps then that literary-ness was born, but there is no mythical event, no offspring of the tradition that tells us of how Pegasus struck, as it were, oil. Ovid makes one feeble attempt, at the beginning of the *Amores* to give us something to remember him by, but it is no Newtonian-Miltonic apple, no serpent with its tail in its mouth, seen in the flickering of a meditative fire, that suggested (or so he said) the construction of the benzene ring to the German chemist Kekulé. No—a mere bit of staging:

> Arma gravi numero violentaque bella parabam
> edere, materia conveniente modis.
> par erat inferior versus—risisse Cupido
> dicitur atque unum surripuisse pedem.

He was preparing to write of battles, of epical subjects in the hexameters proper to their subject, he tells us, but a giggling Cupid filched a foot from the even-numbered lines, and there he was, writing in elegiacs of matters more germane to the concerns of that wee marksman's mama. Hollywood's version of the composition of the "Raindrop" Prelude is as much more probable as it is less artful than this.

The invention of new forms, of course, has its perils as well as its rewards: for every instance of a Psalmist tranquillizing a madly raging Monarch with echoes of pacific flocks and restorative green pastures, there is that of a Terpander, the poet-musician of antiquity who, legend hath it, added three strings to the then-tetrachordal lyre and suffered Olympian wrath in consequence. Marsyas was flayed for playing upon the wind instrument that Athena, glimpsing in a pool the disasters wrought upon her visage by the exigencies of oboe *embouchure*, cast aside with, we may assume, a violent oath. In an iron age there are other disasters, e.g. the neglect by posterity of one's achievement, as witnessed by the case of John Hookham Frere, whose adaptation of the Italian *ottava rima* has been submerged in the flood of Byron's successes with it. Indeed, it might be ventured that if an originator wishes to preserve his claim to a new shaping of the well-wrought urn, he had best put his name, as well as his mind to it.[1]

[1] Indeed, certain scientists have been known to suffer in this way. While Lord Snow will undoubtedly observe that very few heroes of the Other Culture appear in the following pages, the ensuing instance might be noted:

> Pocketa-pocketa
> Ernest Lord Rutherford
> Blushed to confess, as he
> Stared at the floor:
>
> "Protons are vast, glory
> Infinitesimal;
> Sharing one's fame with a
> Dane is a bore!"

JOHN HOLLANDER

There is no danger that the late Edmund Clerihew Bentley will be forgotten as the originator of
the form which bears his name and which we shall
presently consider. Such was the zeal of some
scarcely-needed champions of the sacred name and
memory of Edward Lear that a false-etymology of
"limerick" from an improbable corruption of
"Lear-ic" has occasionally lurked about the scholarly literature. Whoever the seventeenth-century
French lounge-lizard may have been who livened
up the flagging marivaudage of some unseasonably
hot June with the introduction of *bouts rimés*, his
shade may perhaps welcome that anonymity which
he now possesses for us. But in a generous effort to
prevent these leaves of sure obliteration from ob-
scuring the true path of certain recent formal inventions, the editors should like to take this opportu-
nity to salute publicly (perhaps for the first time)
the emergence from the atelier of Mr. James Merrill of two new modes, one lyric, the other more
epigrammatic and of particular relevance to the
present remarks.

Of these, the first is the stanza form of an unpub-
lished volume by various hands, generally known as
the *Balbec Liederbuch*, a collection of songs on

Or, as nôtre cher maître S. J. Perelman has put the
paradigm case of this, "The Alfred Zeigler test, named
after Professor Schaffner of the University of Rochester."

Proustian themes; the lyric form is designed to meet the demands of the melody to which the verses are all sung: the "Colonel Bogie" theme made famous in *The Bridge on the River Kwai*. Thus:

> *Swann's Way* (*pause*)
> A Book by Mar-cel Proust
> Tells how (*pause*)
> Its hero took to roost
> Racy
> Odette de Crécy
> Who to his friends could
> Not be in-
> Troduced.

—which serves as the introductory chorus; or, perhaps, a contribution by one of the present editors:

> Marcel
> You musn't rage like that,
> Charlus'
> Chapeau is squashed all flat!
> Lover,
> You'll soon discover
> What *le Baron's* keep-
> Ing under
> His hat!

Of course it may be objected that this is not really an instance of formal creation, the rhythms of the march (and henceforth how inadequate its merely whistled syncopations will seem!) proposing, the word merely disposing. But as the over-quoted Verlaine reminds us, *"De la musique avant toute chose"*; in any event, the second of the new cadences that have emerged in the past half-decade is unmusical in the extreme, unless one were to be so modish as to proclaim the aleatory and random domains as Euterpe's own. For the actual verse-form is in each instance totally a function of its content, in accordance with the tightest strictures of antiquity, each line being wholly and solely a perfect anagram of the name of a poet, living or dead. For examples one might turn to the shortest and longest of such efforts as are yet in the canon, these being the work of Mr. Merrill's assiduous follower in the genre, Mr. Daryl Hine. It will be noticed that the organic perfection of such a form extends even to the title, which is, not only properly one of the lines of the poem (indeed, in many senses, the *first* one), but its name, description, and extension as well. Thus, the shortest:

LI PO

O lip
poli!
I plo-
P oil.

And the longest:

I, tried for gain? How scales will fall!
Ill fared till crisis, when awe of gaol,
Law scared off heart's wing. I lie, I loll,
Wilt. Eros fled so willing a farce. Hail.

Would that the editors could give some tidily
anecdotal account of the origins of these most recent of inventions. But once again, the elusive instant
of innovation nastily and yet, somehow, prettily
evades capture. It is therefore not merely with a
sense of personal pleasure and pride that the editors
are able to offer here for the first time Mr. Hecht's
account of the origin of the form of the Double
Dactyl in all its circumstantial detail, but with a
greater sense that some redress to the benefit of the
arts in general may accrue, and that in the memories
of future children and their parents the dramatic
locus of this invention may find its proper place.

The Origin of the Form: Mr. Hecht's Account

In September of 1951 I became a Fellow of the
American Academy in Rome. The Academy is a
handsome establishment, offering to Americans

with some distinction in selected disciplines, and to a number of distinguished foreign visitors, those benefits and opportunities with which Napoleon had endowed the Prix de Rome amidst the grandeur of the Villa Medici. I shall not list my colleagues of that time, in order to avoid the appearance of name-dropping, except to say that Ingrid Bergman, (who was not actually a Fellow) used to come over to have Thanksgiving dinner with us, chiefly out of her great fondness for the sculptor, Carl Milles, and perhaps a nostalgia for turkey. The Academy is located on the Janiculum Hill and beside the Aurelian Wall, roughly between the Porta St. Pancrazio and the Aqua Paola.

I had become acquainted with a young classical scholar and his wife, Paul and Naomi Pascal, and by early October they had noticed that I was the only poet in the place; others being devoted to classical studies of various kinds, including archeology, numismatics, and the compiling of accurate Tribune lists; there were as well Fellows in painting, sculpture, musical composition, architecture, art history and landscape architecture. Out of a mixture of genuine interest and politely concealed suspicion, the Pascals asked if they could see some of my work, and I gave them a small sheaf of poems, some of them only just finished. Among them was a poem called *Japan* which I had written some years after serving in the occupation forces there at the end of the Second World War.

This poem is composed of seven stanzas of ten lines each, rather intricately metered and rhymed, after the manner of John Donne or George Herbert. The stanza is made up of three pentameter lines, followed by a trimeter, then two tetrameters, then two pentameters, a trimeter, and a pentameter; and the rhyme scheme goes ABABCCDEDE. The meter is essentially iambic, a poor foot that has perished at the hands of countless innovators and emancipators of poetry since Dr. Williams cast opprobrium upon it.

Doubtless it was fitting that Robert Boyle should have made his initial observations upon shining meat at night when it is dark enough for the phenomenon to be observed; and there is a special glamor about being roused from bed to undertake scientific investigations. It reflects favorably upon the moral character of the scientist, indicating his zeal, and his indifference to personal comfort when curiosity and interest are aroused. And night is good for atmospherics, mysterious and given to gothic storms, such as gave Boyle his bad cold in the nose. I wish I were able to provide such a setting for what I shall now report, but a deep sense of historical fact obliges me to say that no one was peculiarly discomforted by the meeting I had with the Pascals at 11:30 on the morning of November 3rd, in the studio of an artist friend of ours. The weather was pleasant, it was near lunch and we were all hungry, and nobody had colds. The artist had gone out to play tennis.

Japan is an old-fashioned poem. Nevertheless, the Pascals seemed to like it and questioned me about certain details, such as, what the hell was Schistosomiasis Japonica? I was delighted to explain what all soldiers who had been to Japan were richly instructed in: that it was a disease for which there was no cure save one that was also fatal, it was endemic to Japan, and it resulted from the use of their night-soil to fertilize their fields and rice paddies. Having explained this, as well as some other items about the Japanese economy, I proceeded to point out another fact about the poem in which, up to that time, I had taken only a private delight. "It had always been my ambition," I told the Pascals, "to write a poem with a reasonably long line that was one word long, as T. S. Eliot did in 'Mr. Eliot's Sunday Morning Service' which has for its first line, 'Polyphiloprogenitive'. As you see, in my poem *Schistosomiasis* has a line all to itself." There was a pause here as I allowed the Pascals to savor something of my technical skill. And it was then that Paul pointed out to me that while the meter of the poem was essentially iambic, the line I was so

17

pleased with was in fact composed of two dactylic feet. I think I mentioned something about the freedom of Milton's scansion, and Shakespeare's, especially in the later plays.

Now, Naomi Pascal is a sensitive woman, and while Paul was carefully considering the justice of my defense, she detected something crestfallen in my aspect. As she later said, "I detected something crestfallen in your aspect." Diffidently and with unusual kindness, she suggested that if Schistosomiasis did not properly fit this poem, perhaps a new form could be devised to which it would be better suited. Her motives were of the purest, most compassionate sort. She wanted to salvage that word for me and for poetry. And while her generous nature was apparent, the force and importance of her suggestion did not sink in till lunch. For lunch we had: *antipasto*, followed by *lasagna*, *saltimbocca alla romana*, *insalata mista*, and a bottle of good Frascati, and ending with what the Italians wittily call "English soup." I mention these things only because William Empson has recorded a conversation with T. S. Eliot [2] in which Eliot took exception to a

---

[2] "Perhaps the most charming case of his peculiar note, which however wilful in its sadness is always at the opposite pole to malice, occurred when a younger poet (long ago now) published a diary. I should explain that Eliot takes cheese rather seriously; as witness the pro-

report of the kind of cheese he had eaten at lunch with another poet.

It must have been half way through the saltimbocca that Paul and I became alive to the enormous possibilities latent in Naomi's gentle suggestion. So moved were we that we turned instantly, as if governed by a single impulse, to the Frascati. While it is true that nothing memorable was said, it should

---

nouncement, 'I find I can no longer travel except where there is a native cheese. I am therefore bounded, northwards by Yorkshire . . .' and the rest of the points of the compass were all tidy (I think he had a fair run to the south) but I no longer know what they were. The younger poet had recorded a lunch with 'Tom!' at which he had told Tom that simplicity and deep feeling were what made good poetry, and Tom had agreed. This was what gave his own poetry its lasting qualities ('Yes' Tom had said) and on the other hand gave good reason to prophesy that the poetry of Tom would only prove a passing fashion. Tom had seemed much struck by this. Meeting Eliot not long after I made bold to mention the diary, and he said, 'Very interesting. He did me the kindness . . . to send me the proofs . . . of the parts . . . concerning myself.' I said I hoped he had found them all right. His manner became a trifle severe, though not noticeably sadder. 'I found it necessary,' he said, 'in the interests of truth, to correct the name of the cheese.' "

From "The Style of the Master" in *T. S. Eliot*, edited by March and Tambimuttu (London: Editions Poetry, 1948; Chicago: Henry Regnery Co., 1949) Reprinted in *T. S. Eliot*, edited by Kenner (Englewood Cliffs, N.J.: Prentice Hall, Inc., 1962)

be remembered that Bell's famous exclamation was only a response to his own silly clumsiness. Ours was a dignified and pregnant silence, much like Alexander Fleming's when gazing at his mouldy pots. Such moments are hard to describe.

By the end of the afternoon we had hammered out the nature and details of the form. Neither of us could have foreseen, in those early days, the success and celebrity that would attend upon us many years later when the Double Dactyl made its first public appearance in the June, 1966 issue of Esquire. I quote briefly from some correspondence with Professor Pascal, relating to this matter.

> *Dept. of Classics*
> *U. of Washington*
> *Seattle*
> *10 June 1966*

Dear Tony,[3]

I was delighted to get your first postcard (signed Quintus Tertullian) some months ago, reporting the imminence of the explosion onto the unsuspecting world of the double-dactyl movement. I assumed it was from you (aside from other considerations I thought I recognized your typewriter) but since you did not include your address, I let it go until the Es-

---

[3] He calls me Tony. We are old friends.

quire came out. Immediately after I saw that lovely page, I wrote them a long letter, expecting that I would get in touch with you somehow through them. That isn't much of an excuse for not writing to you direct, so I will just ask you to forgive me. (And thank you for including your address this time—ya know what I mean?)

All the activity you now report with Atheneum and Esquire is very exciting. Maybe I will be a full professor next year on the strength of it. I am already treated with much more respect by my students than I used to get when my only publication had been in *Neophilologus*, *Classical Journal*, *Traditio*, and *Studies in Honor of B. L. Ullman*.

To which I responded, in part, as follows:

New York City
June 14, 1966

Dear Paul,

I should think that you were now in a position to *demand* a full professorship. Who do those stingy bastards think they are? How often do they have on their faculty a man directly responsible for a major innovation in poetic form? If they don't give it to you, screw 'em; resign. There will always be a place at Harvard for men of brisk and original invention. You tell your god-damned chairman that I said so.

> Thine evermore, whilst this
> *Schreibmaschine* is to him,
> Leverett Saltonstall

Since I have not heard that Paul has joined the Harvard faculty, I assume he got the professorship to which he was so richly entitled. It is unfortunate to have to say so, but sometimes it is necessary to be assertive and use a little pressure in the academic world.

Die Form an Sich: Names and Naming

Some pages back, the editors passed devotedly but nonetheless hurriedly over the question of the Clerihew, that sublime and perfect mode which does for the personal name what Lear's form of the limerick even with its repeated ultimate line, does for the place-name or attribute. It seems hardly necessary to remind the reader of its construction; of the inevitability with which the utterance of the name results in the general moralization, the observation about life, art, reality and the passing parade.

But even the refreshed memory will surely rejoice in

> Sir Humphry Davy
> Detested gravy.
> He lived in the odium
> Of having discovered sodium.

said instance having been produced by Mr. Bentley at the age of sixteen. Now, it will have been apparent to the discerning reader that Mr. Hecht's narrative concerning the invention of the Double Dactyl is everywhere devoted to the origination of the didactylic essence of the form, as opposed to its didactic substance. Debates among future scholiasts about the heart of the matter may, alas, be all too easily envisaged—about whether the proper disposition of the syllables or the crucial fact of the proper name in the second line constitutes the substance, essence, haecceity, quiddity, inscape or whatever of the whole genre. While remaining unwilling to enter such a dispute, the editors still find it advisable to remark that the *mana* or primitive force attached to names by simpler peoples has never wholly disappeared. The Name of all Names, the great Tetragrammaton itself, could, in the days of the Second Temple, be uttered only once a year, by the High Priest on the Day of Atonement, before prostrate multitudes. The scribal components

of that same Name took on, in the minds of medie-
val mystics, all manner of other powers—that
Name, indeed, whose very meaning is an ancient
mystery, some deeming it a causitive form of the
verb *hayah*, "to be," some of *havah*, "to fall."

The names of mere men have undoubtedly lost
their original power and value. Particularly in
America, where anybody can obviously be named
anything, one seems to feel a certain debasement of
coinage. Consider, for example, the aboriginal in-
habitants of the continent, whose red flesh we have
long since pounded into the earth from which it
sprang, and whose onomastic legacy to us has been a
multitude of polysyllabic nonsense which names
our mountains, rivers, states and cities. Writing
with an unquestioned authority albeit with a tend-
ency to blur tribal distinctions, the author of one
source puts it unequivocally:

> "Names could often be loaned, pawned, or
> even given or thrown away outright; on the
> other hand they might be adopted out of re-
> venge without the consent of the owner. The
> possession of a name was everywhere jealously
> guarded, and it was considered discourteous or
> even insulting to address one directly by it.
> This reticence, on the part of some Indians at
> least, appears to have been due to the fact that

every man, and every thing as well, was sup-
posed to have *a real name which so perfectly
expressed his inmost nature as to be practically
identical with him* . . . [Italics ours] [4]

Lo, the untutored mind, etc. But if it has been at
various times in human history the task of poetry to
do more than merely purify the dialect of the tribe,
assert links with The Tradition and so forth; if the
Imagination is to give life to the dead forms of
thought and speech and so forth; if the first and
best poetry was that of our Common Parent, pad-
ding about his garden and naming the fauna and
flora with an ostensive gesture second only to those
of his own Creator, then surely the Double Dactyl
is no empty vessel, no lifeless mirror, no barren

[4] From *Handbook of American Indians*, ed. F. W. Hodge
(Washington, 1910), II, p. 17. The remainder of the
passage is of more than anthropological interest: "This
name might long remain unknown to all, *even to its
owner*, [italics again ours] but at some critical period in
life it was confidentially revealed to him. It was largely on
account of this sacred character that an Indian commonly
refused to give his proper designation, or, when pressed
for an answer, asked someone else to speak it." The editors
can only contemplate with horror the poetic consequences
of the tradition that one writer observed among some
Athapascan tribes, where a father lost his name as soon
as a male child was born and was henceforth called after
the name of his son: "Sonnets" Shakespeare? "Juvenilia"
Tennyson? "Pauline" Browning?

tower thrusting its cold height disdainfully above green fields. The naming of cats may be, as was once remarked, a Difficult Matter, but the naming of names is a Serious one.

So much, for the time being, at any rate, for names. The didactylic names whose syllables manage to fall upon the sensitive ears of the Muse of this form are borne by those who are no more to be envied than pitied. There, but for an ethnolinguistic accident, go all or any of us: only the members of that fictional African tribe thought by the gossipy and unreliable Herodotus to possess no individual personal names would, of course, be exempt from consideration, a privilege undoubtedly already extended them by the fact of their non-existence. Indeed, one of the present editors narrowly escaped secondary immortalization only because of the over-refined sensibilities of a Parent: who, upon being asked by the boyish editor why he had not been named "Jonathan," replied "Because I didn't want your name to sound like a line of *Evangeline*."

Die Form an Sich: Techniques, Problems

The form itself, as it was determined that November day in Rome, is composed of two quatrains, of which the last line of the first rhymes with the last line of the second. All the lines except the rhyming ones, which are truncated, are composed of two dactylic feet. The first line of the poem must be a double dactylic nonsense line, like "Higgledy-piggledy," or "Pocketa-pocketa" (this last, of course, borrowed from *The Secret Life of Walter Mitty*). The second line must be a double dactylic name. And then, somewhere in the poem, though preferably in the second stanza, and ideally in the antepenultimate line, there must be at least one double dactylic line which is *one word long*. (Foreign languages may be employed, and indeed there is a hope that this form will restore macaronic verse to the dignity it has not enjoyed since the Late Middle Ages.) But, and the beauty of the form consists chiefly in this, once such a double dactylic word has successfully been employed in this verse form, it may never be used again.

Two things follow from this. One: that there must be an approved canon of Double Dactyls by which it may be established what words have already been eliminated. Two: that presently, and probably very soon, the entire supply of double dactylic words in all languages will have been exhausted, bringing the form to its ultimate demise.

It must instantly be pointed out that only the grossest and most rough-hewn sense of the form is conveyed by this brief description. In order to become a part of the official canon, the integrity and high standards of which are judged and maintained by Professor Pascal and the present editors, a poem must exhibit certain felicities of rhythm and style which we, as Regents of the Canon, find it somewhat difficult to state as tersely and explicitly as the strictures that appear above.

For example, while titles are perfectly admissible as part of a name (e.g. Marshal de Beresford, Cardinal Tisserant) and epithets may be allowed if they familiarly accompany some name (e.g., Jupiter Pluvius, Ivan the Terrible) the Regents incline to look suspiciously at random and irresponsible freedom in this direction. By way of illustration it may be said that one poem offered for our inspection concerned "Old Ludwig Wittgenstein." Now Wittgenstein died in Cambridge at the age of 62, which, according to present actuarial standards, is not old. Also, he died in April of 1951, so that it would not be proper to speak of him as one from the remote past, as one might speak of Old Plato or Old Aristotle. Indeed, the only sanction the Regents could find for the use of the word depended upon an affectionate, proprietary tone such as Holden Caulfield adopts towards his younger sister, Phoebe, in calling her "Old Phoebe." After due consideration, it was the decision of the Regents that such a tone was improper with respect to Wittgenstein.

Then there is the delicate problem of hyphens. While the Regents at present feel that hyphens may be used quite freely in this form, they have not yet determined how censorious to be about hyphenated double-dactylic words. A decision on this point is hoped for at our next convocation.[5]

Most difficult of all are the problems raised by diphthongs and elisions. For example, how does one pronounce Raphael? Milton's promiscuity in this matter is scarcely helpful:

[5] Wise money would probably bet against their being admitted. It is only by maintaining rigorous standards that one can, as it were, hope to maintain rigorous standards. It will be a great pity, as well as an enviable moral lesson not too easily available, when examples such as the following, by Mr. Richard Howard, have to be otherwise regrettably removed from the canon:

> Higgledy-piggledy
> Mendelssohn-Bartholdy
> Wavered from Ossian to
> Shakespeare to Bach;
>
> Doubtless a form of con-
> Version hysteria
> Conned this poor Jew to the
> Lutheran crock.

It may have been that Mr. Howard, already carried away by the zeal of his studies in the German Romantics, may have been finally done in here by the hyphenation of his subject's name, finding it necessary to repeat the event later on.

Say Goddess, what ensued when Raphael
PARADISE LOST, *Bk. VII–1.40*

'Raphael,' said he, 'thou hear's what stir on Earth
PARADISE LOST, *Bk. V–1.224*

Milton seems to show in his desire to have it both ways the sort of foppish self-indulgence we properly associate with the Cavalier Poets, and it may well be, though neither E. M. W. Tillyard nor Douglas Bush has ventured to suggest it, that Milton may have been a secret royalist, and possibly hard of hearing.

It is to such delicate matters as these[6] that the Regents normally address themselves at their regular meetings, which take place at Le Pavillon, in a soothing and meditative atmosphere that is conducive to high thought. As a consequence of their most recent and fruitful meeting, from which they are only now recovering, they herewith present the

[6] And others; yes, there are others. For example, not to put too fine a point on it, the frequent use of the adverbial formed from the five-syllabled adjective seems a finky way out of a difficulty—not the finkiness of either Falstaff or Hotspur, nor of one who cheats, even, at solitaire, but of one who always elects to play that kind of patience which will work out with a minimum of cheating. Mr. W. H. Auden, having been consulted upon the matter, ruled out, with the iron will of an eighteenth-century prosodist, all such constructions.

Official Canon as it stands as of the date subscribed below, in historical order of their protagonists, with all doubtful cases, duplications and other disputable matter duly accounted for in the notes and such scholarly apparatus as has been deemed fitting.

ANTHONY HECHT

JOHN HOLLANDER

New York, December, 1966

DOUBLE DACTYLS

PARADISE LOST, BOOK V
AN EPITOME

Higgledy-piggledy
Archangel Raphael,
Speaking of Satan's re-
Bellion from God:

"Chap was decidedly
Tergiversational,
Given to lewdness and
Rodomontade."

ANTHONY HECHT

Higgledy-piggledy
Homo Neanderthal
Coming from crowded caves
Onto the scene

Viewed all the countryside
Anthropomorphically—
Rather surrealist,
That must have been.

CHRISTOPHER WALLACE-CRABBE

Higgledy-piggledy
Father * Methuselah
Set an example to
Settle our fears,

Being so splendidly
Ungeriatrically
Antediluvian
All of those years.

CHRISTOPHER WALLACE-CRABBE

* Clearly an epithet, not a name; yet just as clearly that of
a Patriarch. A graver problem arises with the question of
chronological placement: should he precede or follow the
Neanderthal troglodyte? The reader will observe that a
strong, Higher-Critical line has been taken here.

Patty-cake, patty-cake,
Marcus Antonius
What do you think of the
African Queen?

Gubernatorial
Duties require my
Presence in Egypt. Ya
Know what I mean?

PAUL PASCAL

Patty-cake, patty-cake,
Jupiter Pluvius,
Antediluvian
Rain-making chap,

Showered his masculine
Potentialities
All over Danae's
Succulent lap.

ANTHONY HECHT

Higgledy-piggledy
Herod Antipater
After the Dance, had the
Lunch-table set:

"Balletomania,
Bah! I just wanted a
Nice dish of *tête de pro-*
Phète, vinaigrette."

JOHN HOLLANDER

Higgledy-piggledy
Judas Iscariot,
Cloven of palate, of
Voice insecure,

Mumbler and lisper, was
Hypocoristically
Known to his buddies as
"Jude, the Obscure."

ANTHONY HECHT

ABOVE ALL THAT?

Higgledy-piggledy
Mary of Magdala
Said to the dolorous
Mother of God:

"Parthenogenesis
I for one left to the
Simple amoeba or
Gasteropod."

JAMES MERRILL

PROFESSIONALISM

Higgledy-piggledy,
Quintus Tertullian
Drew on his Rhetoric
With his last breath,

(Sesquipedalian
Valedictorian)
Boring his near ones and
Dear ones to death.

ANTHONY HECHT

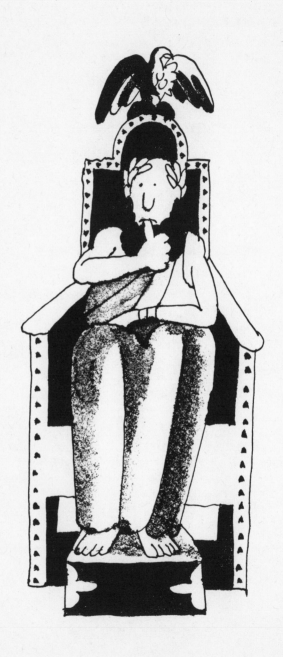

POINT OF VIEW

Higgledy-piggledy
Marcus Aurelius
Guiding his life by a
Stark rule of thumb,

Garnered the nickname of
"Impermeabile" *
Meaning both "Stoic," and,
Possibly, "dumb."

ANTHONY HECHT

* *Impermeabile* pronounced, of course, in the Italian manner.

Higgledy-piggledy
Heliogabalus *
Lurched through the Forum, his
Bottom a-wag,

Vainly pretending to
Gynaecological
Problems beneath his Im-
Perial drag.

JOHN HOLLANDER

* "It may seem probable, the vices and follies of Elagabalus
have been adorned by fancy, and blackened by prejudice.
Yet confining ourselves to the public scenes displayed before the Roman people, and attested by grave and con-
temporary historians, their inexpressible infamy surpasses
that of any other age or country. The license of an eastern
monarch is secluded from the eye of curiosity by the in-
accessible walls of his seraglio. The sentiments of honour
and gallantry have introduced a refinement of pleasure, a
regard for decency, and a respect for public opinion, into
the modern courts of Europe; but the corrupt and opulent
nobles of Rome gratified every vice that could be col-
lected from the mighty conflux of nations and manners.
Secure of impunity, careless of censure, they lived without
restraint in the patient and humble society of their slaves
and parasites. . . ." (GIBBON's *note*)

Higgledy-piggledy
Tristram of Lyonesse
Gave up the ghost to *la*
Chanson des Anges,

Cheating, at once, of his
Corporeality,
Ysolt Mains-blanches; also
Ysolt, Blancmange.*

JOHN HOLLANDER

* i.e. the other Ysolt.

Moishele, Moishele
Moses Maimonides,
Bowing and chanting "Bar-
Uch Adonai,"

Picked up the telephone
Anachronistically,
Ordered pastrami with
Mustard on rye.

ERIC SALZMAN

1066

Higgledy-piggledy
William the Conqueror
Landed at Pevensey,
Solid and sly,

Thickened the native tongue
Polysyllabically,
Gave to the monarchy
One in the eye.

CHRISTOPHER WALLACE-CRABBE

TROU BAD!

> Higgledy-piggledy
> Richard Plantagenet
> Sailed off for France, full of
> Oedipal scorn:
>
> "Erotogenesis
> Can't be *all* mythic, if
> Mother still makes it with
> Bertrand de Born." *

JOHN HOLLANDER

* "Dante Alighieri put this man in hell for that he was a stirrer up of strife.
Eccovi!
Judge ye!
Have I dug him up again?"

(EZRA POUND'S *note*)

Higgledy-piggledy,
Wolfram von Eschenbach
Chanted aloud (while we
Sat on a bench)

Tedious persiflage,
Stolen * (as shown by the
Urquellenforschungen)
All from the French.

JOHN HOLLANDER

* The Regents are in complete agreement on this, and one
of them is particularly delighted with "persiflage."

Higgledy-piggledy
Matthias Grünewald
Got a commission for
Something in Oils.

(Dermatological
Clinics need altars) so
Jesus got measles and
Pustulent boils.

JOHN HOLLANDER

Higgledy-piggledy
Pico Mirandola
In the Academy
Works with a will;

With what a verve he gets
Neoplatonical
Since a philanthropist's
Footing the bill!

CHRISTOPHER WALLACE-CRABBE

"Higgledy-piggledy
Andrea Doria
Lives in the name of this
Glorious boat.

As I sit writing these
Non-navigational
Verses a—CRASH! BANG! BLURP!
GLUB". . . (end of quote).

JOHN HOLLANDER

Higgledy-piggledy
Nic'laus * Copernicus
Looked at the Universe,
Spoke to the throng:

Give up your Ptolemy,
Rise up and follow me,
Heliocentrically
Ptolemy's wrong.

NANCY L. STARK

* This is clearly cheating; on the other hand, "Nicky"
would have been far, far worse. Lines 5 and 6 are nevertheless inspired.

Higgledy-piggledy
Titus Andronicus,
Fitting himself to the
Classical clime,

Covered his belly with
Decalcomanias
Picturing passionate
Sexual crime.

ANTHONY HECHT

Higgledy-piggledy
Juliet Capulet
Cherished the tenderest
Thoughts of a rose:

"What's in a name?" said she,
Etymologically,
"Save that all Montagues
Stink in God's nose."

ANTHONY HECHT

Higgledy-piggledy
Herbert of Cherbury
Had a kid brother who
Took to the cloth;

They were (to speak of them
UnMetaphysically)
One a dark butterfly,
One a bright moth.

CHRISTOPHER WALLACE-CRABBE

Higgledy-piggledy
Don Juan Tenorio
Tempted his girl with a
Garlic bouquet.

Stink diabolical,
Aphrodisiacal
Put her in heat but it
Drove him away.

ERIC SALZMAN

Higgledy-piggledy
Mme. de Maintenon *
Shouted, "Up yours!" when ap-
Proached for the rent,

And, in her anger, pro-
Ceeded to demonstrate,
Iconographically,
Just what she meant.

ANTHONY HECHT

* "On the King's death she retired altogether to St. Cyr.
It is surprising that the king left her almost nothing; he
simply recommended her to the care of the Duke of
Orleans."

VOLTAIRE, *The Age of Louis XIV*

Higgledy-piggledy
Madame de Pompadour
Muttered with fear, *"Il faut
Chercher réfuge."*

Louis replied to her,
Characteristically,
*"Tais-toi, chèrie, après
Moi, le déluge."*

E. WILLIAM SEAMAN

Higgledy-piggledy,
Ditters von Dittersdorf
Hoped that his symphonies
Really would please;

Caconomasia
Ruined him, though, with a
Name that resembled some
Nervous disease.

JOHN HOLLANDER

Higgledy-piggledy
President Jefferson
Gave up the ghost on the
Fourth of July.

So did John Adams, which
Shows that such patriots
Propagandistically
Knew how to die.

ARTHUR W. MONKS

Jacobin-Jacobin
Citizen Robespierre
Died on the guillotine
Cursing the day,

Leaving his rep up to
Historiography,
Sparing us yet a third
Bad German play.

JOHN HOLLANDER

Higgledy-piggledy
Josephine Bonaparte,
Painted by Prud'hon with
Serious mien:

Sorrow? Oh, hardly. Just
Cosmetological
Prudence (her teeth were a
Carious green.*)

JOHN HOLLANDER

* Historical.

Higgledy-piggledy
Ludwig van Beethoven
Scornful of cheer,* and of
Hearing forlorn,

Spitefully hissing, sat
Writing unplayable
Pianississississimo
Notes for the horn.

JOHN HOLLANDER

* Beethoven is never portrayed in a lighter mood. Viz:
     Higgledy-piggledy
     Ludwig van Beethoven
     Bored by requests for some
     Music to hum,

     Finally answered with
     Oversimplicity,
     "Here's my Fifth Symphony:
     Duh, duh, duh, DUM!"

E. WILLIAM SEAMAN

Higgledy-piggledy
Friedrich von Hardenberg
Smiled, as Novalis, when
Sophie turned dank,

Parachromatical
Mix-ups accounted for
Blue mignonette and a
Mariage blanc.*

RICHARD HOWARD

* Something of a cheat, requiring a French pronunciation of "*mariage*" and an English one of "*blanc*." Clearly, the only solution is to read the whole in as thick a German accent as possible, preferably that of the South.

71

Higgledy-piggledy
Klemens von Metternich
Whispered to Talleyrand
Over their drinks,

"Schnitzels around here are
Not what they used to be.*
Abendlandsuntergang.
Everything stinks."

ANTHONY HECHT

* It is clear that Metternich, who, with Kirk, Burke and
Hare is the very model of a conservative, in certain moods
felt that there was little enough to conserve.

Higgledy-piggledy
Baron von Munchausen
Hot for hyperbole
Said, "Listen, babe,

What's with this *nebishe*
Verisimilitude?
Give me the Burroughs Boys,
William and Abe!" *

ANTHONY HECHT

---

* The Baron, unfamiliar with English, labored under the impression that William Burroughs and Abe Burrows spelled their surnames the same way. Indeed, he may have thought of them as a firm or a team like the Smith, Brooks or Marx brothers.

Higgledy-piggledy
Joseph von Eichendorff
Translated Calderòn,
Relished his theme:

Constant commitment to
Deutscheswaldeinsamkeit
Must have convinced him that
Life is a dream.

RICHARD HOWARD

Higgledy-piggledy
Ralph   Waldo   Emerson
Wroth at Bostonian,
Cowardly hints,

Wrote an unprintable
Epithalamion
Based on a volume of
Japanese prints.

ANTHONY HECHT

Higgledy-piggledy
Hans Christian Andersen
Sat with some tow-headed
Lads on a shelf,

Mythopoetically
Hoping that fairy-tales
Aided in keeping his
Hans to himself.

JOHN HOLLANDER

Higgledy-piggledy
Alfred, Lord Tennyson,*
Sternly Victorian,
Muttered in hate,

"Shelley's deplorable
'Epipsychidion'
Fosters our growing de-
Linquency rate."

ANTHONY HECHT

* Or, in a coarser vein:
       Higgledy-piggledy
       Alfred, Lord Tennyson
       Walked round his garden, in-
       Toning his vowels,

       Paused, then apologised:
       "Dicotyledonous
       Beans do the *windiest*
       Things to one's bowels!"

JOHN HOLLANDER

Higgledy-piggledy
Emily Dickinson
Flew to the cupola
Where she could write:

"Though it's a bore I am
Heterosexual:
Murder and incest are
Sweetness and light."

DONALD HALL

Higgledy-piggledy,
Benjamin Harrison,
Twenty-third President,
Was, and, as such,

Served between Clevelands, and
Save for this trivial
Idiosyncracy,
Didn't do much.

JOHN HOLLANDER

Higgledy-piggledy
Thomas A. Edison
Turned on a switch with a
Wave of his wand,

Giving his name to some
Organizational
Chaps in whose light we are
Now being Conned.

SALLY BELFRAGE

Higgledy-piggledy
Rodya Raskolnikov
Belted two dames with a
Broad-bladed ax.

"I am the wictim * of
Misericordia,
Beaten," said he, "by re-
Legion and sax."

ANTHONY HECHT

* Dialectologists will undoubtedly be offended by this, as no Russian-speaker would ever so distort the voiced labial fricative "v"; however, it must be remembered that the dialect here spoken is Standard Middle Hollywood Central European.

Higgledy-piggledy
Empress Victoria
Answered when asked to give
Gladstone the nod,

"Screw that old Aryan
Parliamentarian!
Dizzy and I stand for
Britain and God."

E. WILLIAM SEAMAN

Higgledy-piggledy
Anna Karenina
Went off her feed and just
Couldn't relax,

Then, quite ignoring the
Unsuitability,
Threw in the sponge and was
Scraped off the tracks.

JOHN HOLLANDER

Higgledy-piggledy
Ossip Gabrilovich,
Answered, when asked, "How did
So-and-so play?"

"Save for wrong notes, he was
Quasi-acceptable.*
You'll get no gossip from
Ossip today."

E. WILLIAM SEAMAN

* This is what a logician would call a self-descriptive
word, like "word," "English," "Polysyllabic" and so forth.
See *Introduction* on hyphenation.

Higgledy-piggledy
Joseph Djugashvili
Showed, with his pipe and his
Flowing Moustache,

Anti-revisionist
Irritability,
Making some comrades break
Out in a rash.

JOHN HOLLANDER

Higgledy-piggledy
Franklin D. Roosevelt
High over Jutland flew
In from the East;

"Well," Quipped a Minister
Plenipotentiary,
"*Something* is Groton in
Denmark, at least!"

JOHN HOLLANDER

Higgledy-piggledy
Hugo von Hofmannsthal
Mused on the day of his
Son's suicide:

"Surely a kind of ob-
Scure mystic sympathy—
Hapsburgersschicksalslied—
Calls me," and died.

RICHARD HOWARD

Higgledy-piggledy
Hugh Selwyn Mauberley
Chiselled some poetry—
Or was it Pound?

No one can tell for sure
But it would seem to be
Incontrovertibly
Doubly profound.

CHRISTOPHER WALLACE-CRABBE

Higgledy-piggledy
Ludwig Mies Van der Rohe
Softly complained to the
Heavenly host,

"Buckminster Fuller says
Dodecahedronals
Carry stress better than
Lintel and post."

ANTHONY HECHT

Higgledy-piggledy
Thomas Stearns Eliot *
Wrote dirty limericks
Under the rose,

Using synecdoches,
Paranomasias,
Zeugmas, and rhymes he de-
Plored in his prose.

ANTHONY HECHT

* Mr. Wallace-Crabbe, however, had this to add:
Higgledy-piggledy
Thomas Stearns Eliot
Made a whole poem to
Carry one word.

What was it now? *Poly-*
Philoprogenitive.
I do not like it. I
Think it absurd.

Higgledy-piggledy
Dorothy Richardson
Wrote a huge book with her
Delicate muse

Where (though I hate to seem
Uncomplimentary)
Nothing much happens and
Nobody screws.

JOHN HOLLANDER

IMPRESSIONISM

Fiddlesky diddlesky
Vladimir Nabokov
Pared his perceptions down
Beautifully fine,

Firmly insisting on
UnDostoevskian
Flickers of color and
Tremors of line.

CHRISTOPHER WALLACE-CRABBE

Higgledy-piggledy
J. Press and Company
Gave me the darkest of
Corporate looks,

Writing me off, when I
Passed by their shop, as some
Tatterdemalion
Trousered by Brooks.

JOHN HOLLANDER

CONFESSION

> Patty-cake, patty-cake,
> Vladimir Horowitz
> Took up the cymbals, and
> Said,* with an air,
>
> "Diese unmögliche
> Hammerklaviersmusik
> Soll ich night spielen, ich
> Find' sie zu schwer."

ANTHONY HECHT

* Vladimir Horowitz speaks several languages, all of them fluently.

Higgledy-piggledy
Victor Emmanuel
Whined to Francisco, "It's
Not at all fair.

Why can't I too be a
Generalissimo?
Surely Benito has
Costumes to spare."

E. WILLIAM SEAMAN

POINT OF VIEW

> Higgledy-piggledy
> Christopher Isherwood
> Looked on Berlin with a
> Camera's eye,
>
> But when his faith became
> NeoDravidian
> Hollywood lenses would
> Moisten and cry.

CHRISTOPHER WALLACE-CRABBE

Higgledy-piggledy
Laurence Olivier
Faced a dilemma,
As some were aware.

Heeding the dictates of
Practicability,
How can you Plowright with
Vivien there?

E. WILLIAM SEAMAN

Higgledy-piggledy
Arthur M. Schlesinger,
Asked, "How does Washington
Do without you?"

Answered, "It suffers from
Counterintelligence,
High on consensus, but
Low on I.Q."

E. WILLIAM SEAMAN

Higgledy-piggledy
Robert C. Rauschenberg
Gunked up his canvas with
All kinds of glop.

"Though mixing media
Meta-linguistically
Seems to me silly I
Can't seem to stop."

ERIC SALZMAN

Higgledy-piggledy
Robert F. Kennedy,
Scoring apartheid, pro-
Duced a sage quote,

Grinning a grin rather
Machiavellian:
"Who in New York needs the
Afrikaans vote?"

E. WILLIAM SEAMAN

Higgledy-piggledy
David Ben-Gurion
Said to *Der Alte*, "We're
Both on the rocks.

How they ignore us is
Incomprehensible.
Pfui on youth. Have some
Bagel and lox."

E. WILLIAM SEAMAN

Higgledy-piggledy
Gustav von Aschenbach,
Fed to the gullet with
High German joys,

Sought in an atmosphere
Mediterranean
Soft, antinomian
Decadent boys.

ANTHONY HECHT

Higgledy-piggledy
John Simon Guggenheim,
Honored wherever the
Muses collect,

Save in the studies (like
Mine) which have suffered his
Unjustifiable,
Shocking neglect.

JOHN HOLLANDER

Higgledy-piggledy
Jacqueline Kennedy
Went back to Hydra and
Found it a mess—

Neon lights, discotheques . . .
"Landlord, what's *hap*pening?"
"'Ανθρωπιστήκαμε*
Go home, U.S."

JAMES MERRILL

* or, roughly, "We have become human beings!"

Jiggery-pokery
President Kennedy
Chose, in the White House,
A Canopied bed—

One that was used by his
Philoprogenitive
Grandfather Bobby and
Great-uncle Ted.

JOHN HOLLANDER

FINN AGAIN *

Ibbety bibbety
Anna L. Plurabelle
rivering seaward par
swerve and per bend,

lapsed, till rejoyceaments
philolinguistical
mythed her and founded her,
words without end.

IRMA BRANDEIS

* The placement in chronological order here poses grave problems.

ANGUISH

> Higgledy-piggledy
> Christopher Wallace-Crabbe
> Tripped over dactyls on
> Tentative toes.
>
> O, how he hankered for
> Hendecasyllables,
> Double sestinas or
> Senecan prose!

CHRISTOPHER WALLACE-CRABBE

VALE

Pocketa, pocketa,
Bard of ill omen,* I
Hereby renounce the
Poetical life.

I've been forgetting my
Altertumswissenschaft,
Losing my sleep, and neg-
Lecting my wife.

PAUL PASCAL

* An exceptional case, which the Regents feel must be incorporated in the canon, despite the lack of a proper double-dactylic name, because of the lovely echo of Poe. "Bard of ill omen" is in the vocative case, by the way, addressed, presumably, to Mr. Hecht. See *Introduction*.

Higgledy-piggledy
Anthony Hollander,
Two-bards-in-one, worked their
Brains to a storm,

Seeking out words for the
Antepenultimate
Line of this dismally
Difficult form.

JOHN HOLLANDER